LEWESDON HILL

1788

WILLIAM CROWE

Introduction

JAMES CROWDEN

FLAGON PRESS

2007

Lewesdon Hill was first published anonymously in 1788
by The Clarendon Press, Oxford

Second edition with William Crowe identified as the author,
also published by The Clarendon Press Oxford 1788

Third edition with other poems published in 1804
by T Cadell and W Davies. London

Fourth edition with other poems published by John Murray 1827
Fifth edition Woodstock Press 1989

This edition with Introduction by James Crowden 2007

Published by The Flagon Press
Whitelackington
Designed by Andrew Crane
Printed in Milborne Port by Remous Ltd
Introduction © James Crowden 2007

James Crowden is hereby identified as the author
of the Introduction and asserts his moral rights

Hand-coloured etching of William Crowe by Robert Dighton
courtesy of National Portrait Gallery, London 1808

A CIP record for this book is available from the British Library

ISBN   978-0-9557073-0-8

A CELEBRATED PUBLIC ORATOR.

WILLIAM CROWE

Introduction: William Crowe and *Lewesdon Hill*

William Crowe was born in Midgham, Berkshire, between Newbury and Aldermaston Wharf in the valley of the Kennet and was christened on 8th October 1745. His father, a carpenter, worked in Winchester. William was a very gifted child; his talent was soon spotted and he was whisked off to Winchester College. In 1758 he was elected a 'poor scholar' and also became a chorister in Winchester College chapel. In 1764, at 19, he was fifth on the roll for New College, Oxford and once again excelled himself. (There were long-standing connections between Winchester College and New College because both had been founded by William of Wycombe, 1320-1404.) It seems highly probable that Crowe's early education was helped financially and furthered in other ways by Jonathan Shipley, Bishop of St Asaph, not least because *Lewesdon Hill* is dedicated to the bishop in fulsome terms. Jonathan Shipley was well connected, in those days always a help, a Whig who developed a strong opposition to George III's policies towards the American Colonies. In addition, William Crowe developed a lifelong friendship with the bishop's son, William Davies Shipley, who like himself had been born in Midgham in 1745.

At New College William Crowe became a tutor, gained a degree in law, and in 1773 was made a Fellow, a position he held till 1783. He was also ordained. After one particularly fine sermon in 1782 he was presented by New College with the living of Stoke Abbott in West Dorset, a small but remarkably pleasant rural backwater near Beaminster. It was here that he wrote *Lewesdon Hill*, a poem about the large hill which dominates the village. The views from Lewesdon are still stunning, despite its present-day clothing of beech (in William's time the summit was 'furze-clad') – they take in the Marshwood Vale and the Dorset coast as far as Bridport, right down to the borders with Devon. As noted in the original Advertisement to the 1788 edition, the hill is often twinned with its neighbour Pilsdon Pen. Sailors called the pair 'the Cow and Calf' and used them as leading marks when out fishing or sailing in Lyme Bay.

Lewesdon Hill, published anonymously by the Clarendon Press in 1788, runs to some 524 lines of blank verse and describes a walk up the hill from Stoke Abbott on a fine May morning. It received high praise and was reprinted the same year, this time giving William Crowe's name as author. William Lisle Bowles called it 'the most sublime loco-descriptive poem in the English language', and Samuel Moore considered it 'the best piece of blank verse since the days of Milton'. What is perhaps more interesting is that Azariah Pinney showed *Lewesdon Hill* to William Wordsworth in November 1795, just two months after William and his sister Dorothy had moved in to Racedown House, near Birdsmoorgate. (Wordsworth was tutor to Azariah's son.) And it seems that in March 1795, while he was in Bristol, Samuel Taylor Coleridge had also read the poem, though it was to be a year or two before he came to stay at Racedown, in June 1797. No doubt he and the two Wordsworths then walked the spine of Pilsdon Pen together, taking Lewesdon Hill in their stride as they relived Crowe's May morning, less than ten years after the poem was written. No doubt, too, that the scenery became even more serene after a few drops of the old tincture…

Lewesdon Hill can thus be seen not only as a fine expansive poem in its own right, with much local detail, but also as an important precursor to several of Wordsworth's and Coleridge's works. Both poets derived something from it, not just from its lyrical passages, which are quite delightful, but also from its political, libertarian, even pro-republican sentiments. As Professor Jonathan Wordsworth points out in his 1989 Introduction to the poem, *Lewesdon Hill* was in Wordsworth's library and is mentioned in his 1820 Postcript to the River Duddon sonnets. Some critics say it also leads into the Tintern Abbey and Wye Valley poems of 1798. It is clear that both Wordsworth and Coleridge found the work an inspiration, a major landmark on their horizon whilst they were out at sea. Or as Jonathan Wordsworth put it so succinctly: 'If Crowe in 1788 could not himself quite see the promised land, his poem is of undeniable importance to those who did.' *Lewesdon Hill* showed Wordsworth what could be done with landscape. A Dorset prelude.

It was at just this time, around 1795, that Dorothy Wordsworth was having a significant effect on her brother, encouraging him through her keen and feminine observations of nature to choose poetry as his medium. For those who know the area well, a tantalising sidetrack is that below Racedown, to one side of the road leading down to Bettiscombe, is a valley which until recently contained a whole host of wild daffodils. I do not know what the local farmer has done to them, but if he was in any way responsible for their vanishing, then he should be held accountable! Until ten years ago you could see the whole valley covered in yellow, and it was a fine place for a children's picnic. People came from miles around to see this wonder of West Dorset. Vandalism and modern agriculture writ large; fertiliser and sprays versus poetry.

Like Dorothy, William Crowe was a keen observer of nature and could read the landscape. Lewesdon Hill and its surroundings are his Parnassus, his Mount

Olympus, where the hills and vales are clothed in poets, sheep and shepherds. The home of his muse. At Stoke Abbot at the foot of the hill not far from the church, is a sacred spring and alongside it lives one of Dorset's oldest men Jim Webber, still working at the ripe old age of 104. An oracle of local wisdom if ever there was one. The nymphs on Lewesdon these days are more likely to be in the saddle and wearing T shirts and hard hats, or else they have migrated into the fleshpots of Bridport and Weymouth… For damsels in distress William Crowe turned to the account of the wreck of the *Halsewell*, a richly laden East Indiaman of 750 tons which had come to grief on the cliffs near Worth Matravers in a bitter storm on the night of January 4th–5th 1786. The ship hit the cliff beam-on and was wedged in the mouth of a large cave between St Aldhelm's Head and Peveril Point. The harrowing stories of the survivors and the tale of Captain Pierce, his two daughters and several nieces who all drowned, along with 160 others, profoundly shocked the nation. The Captain and his nephew could have saved themselves, but stayed on board and comforted the ladies in their hour of need. The young women and Captain Pierce perished in the waves. Out of about 230 only 70 survived. Two men climbed the cliff at night and raised the alarm. The following day those that were still alive in the cave were rescued by Purbeck quarrymen with ropes.

Sadly this description held a premonition of sorrow for William Wordsworth: just ten years after he first read *Lewesdon Hill*, his own brother came to grief off the very same coast in a similar storm on 5th February 1805. John Wordsworth was captain of a large East Indiaman, the *Earl of Abergavenny*, which was lost one and a half miles off Weymouth on the Shambles reef whilst under guidance from a pilot. John Wordsworth and 270 others lost their lives. Many are buried in an unmarked pit in Wyke Regis graveyard. It was a double blow for William Wordsworth – his family had invested heavily in the ship's cargo to provide funds for his poetry. How these images of wrecked East Indiamen must have played on Wordsworth's mind.

But William Crowe was not just interested in recent wrecks; he was also a connoisseur of smuggling techniques and familiar with some of the art and craft practised by the villagers of Burton Bradstock, just a few miles east of Bridport and West Bay: the decoy fires, the warning signals and the cunning trick of sinking barrels under water linked together by a rope to be retrieved later, an old trick but skilfully done, as was the doubling back to France to lure the Customs away. These small 'smuggling' barrels were called 'ankers' and held about 9 gallons so that men could carry them ashore easily. The smuggling tactics of the Dorset fishermen were renowned and for centuries they played their game of cat-and-mouse with the Revenue men.

One of the most notorious smugglers on this coast at the time was Isaac Gulliver, who was born in Wiltshire in 1745, an exact contemporary of William Crowe. Gulliver's name was often associated with Burton Bradstock, and by 1776 so wealthy had he become that he was able to buy the local hillfort, Eggardon Hill, as a landmark for his ships. He planted a small group of trees on its summit to make it more prominent still, but the Revenue men cut them down. How unsporting. (Crowe mentions Eggardon Hill, but dared not do so in relation to the darker arts of smuggling.) Isaac Gulliver kept about 40 men on his books and they who wore smock-frocks and powdered hair from which they acquired the name 'White Wigs'. He amassed a large fortune and eventually decided to retire under an amnesty in 1782, the year William Crowe came to Stoke Abbott. Isaac gave up smuggling tea and brandy and thenceforth concentrated on wine. In 1788, the year of the publication of *Lewesdon Hill*, the Revenue recognised Gulliver as a worthy adversary, referring to him as a person of 'great speculating genius'. This King of the Smugglers died in 1822. No wonder William Crowe was fascinated and that he makes several sly references to brandy and the French coast. (The 'Norman isles' referred to in the poem are of course the Channel Islands favoured haunt of smugglers ; *Lewesdon Hill* is laced with classical allusions and references; the Hellespont, Xerxes, Troy.)

It may even be that one of William's duties was to oversee the delivery of smuggled brandy to his parish and thence to New College cellars. He was a useful man to have on your side and not surprisingly the Fellows always elected him college woodman. His rural knowledge came in handy in timber deals and also in grain sales from glebe land and tithes. (Much of the wealth of Oxford colleges was derived from landholdings.) He himself held two fields in Stoke Abbott and was well acquainted with the farming community and its characters.

In *Lewesdon Hill* William Crowe mentions a certain farmer-philanthropist called Thomas Hollis, 1720-1774, who at one time owned 700 acres in the neighbouring parishes of Corscombe and Halstock. Hollis was strongly connected with Harvard University. His great-uncle had been one of the university's original benefactors along with John Harvard. Thomas continued his great-uncle's tradition of sending out donations and books which he had had reprinted specially, often decorated with libertarian symbols. But Thomas also left his mark on Dorset, renaming all his farms and even fields after philosophers, poets and writers. Hence the farms are called

Liberty, Locke, Harvard, Neville, Marvell, Sydney and Ludlow. The field-names are even more intriguing and read like a compendium of bizarre lecture titles: Confucius, Pythagoras, Aristotle, Plato and Socrates, Lay Preacher, Cassius, Brutus, Oxford, Plato, Reasonableness, Understanding, Comprehension, Toleration, Revolution, William III, Massachusetts, Stuart Coppice, Free State, Commonwealth, Pym, Hampden, Geneva, Bern and January 30th which was the date of Charles 1st's execution. Likewise Stuart Coppice was so called because every seven years hazel has to be cut down to size.

Such wit and wisdom survives to this day in the parishes of Halstock and Corscombe. Who says politics and poetry don't go hand in hand with agriculture? How confusing for farm labourers: 'I'll see you in Pythagoras with five gallons of cider once I've finished scything Massachusetts.' Thomas Hollis always wanted to live in Lyme Regis and it was his idea to make the esplanade on the shore that we see today.

Thomas Hollis died as he was giving orders to his farmworkers. Acting on his previous instructions, they buried him in a hole ten feet deep in one of his fields and then ploughed over so there was no trace. Which field-name did he choose, I wonder? William Crowe, being an earthy man, obviously approved of this 'untitled sepulchre'.

By a curious twist of fate Hollis lives on in America. At Harvard University, **HOLLIS** now stands for the **H**arvard **On**-**L**ine **L**ibrary **I**nformation **S**ystem. Book retrieval – of books which Thomas Hollis may well have sent over himself. (All that learning leads to revolution.) There is even a Hollis Hall, a Hollis Professor of Divinity and a Hollis Professor of Mathematicks and Natural Philosophy. In Dorset we have just a field and a farm: Hollis and Harvard.

Another point of interest: *Lewesdon Hill* sits on the cusp between two very different ages and styles of poetry, the Augustan and the Romantic. Crowe forms a link between the Augustan, neo-classical tradition where reason prevails and the later Romantic poetry where emotion and landscape become inextricably intertwined. In other words his poem provides a valuable stepping-stone between the two traditions. Thomas Hollis and his cousin Timothy Hollis were also governors of a Dissenting school at Litton Cheney. Education was very much on their mind.

But what of the man himself? The more you get to know William Crowe the more appealing he becomes. In 1788, the year *Lewesdon Hill* was published, he exchanged Stoke Abbott for a more lucrative living at Alton Barnes, near Pewsey in Wiltshire. This was presumably in order to be nearer Oxford, where in 1784 he had been made Public Orator for the university. He was often to be seen walking between Oxford and Alton Barnes on foot, a distance of about 40 miles as the crow flies, no doubt composing his sermons and lectures as he went. There are various accounts of him striding between his parishes and the spires of Oxford with a stick and bag slung over his shoulder like an itinerant journeyman, relishing sitting outside rustic pubs as he brushes up his latest discourse. He was said to be a great smoker and would often be seen smoking a long clay pipe on his way into church; he would then lay the pipe down on the communion table whilst he took the service. His students obviously liked his down-to-earth approach and learnt a great deal from him, not just about the classics but about life. As his obituary recorded in 1829, 'As a tutor he filled that situation for many years with ability and success; his manner, as little marked by the repulsive distance, as his instruction was by the pedantry, of other lecturers, soon acquired for him the attachment and affection of his pupils.' An earlier version of Seamus Heaney, perhaps?

In the role of rustic at Oxford, Crowe played his audience marvellously. Thomas Frognal Dibdin, writing in the *Gentleman's Magazine* in 1836, says of him: 'With Professor Crowe, of New College, I had the pleasure of a long rather than of an intimate acquaintance. But I saw and knew enough of him to assure me of the warmth of his heart and the attainments of his head, as well as of the extreme simplicity of his manners and address. Perhaps no man who wore the academic gown so long and so constantly, ever suffered so little of the rust of a rural life to be worn off…He was of all men one of the most original in his habits and modes of expression, and of a spirit so meek and gentle, that he would not, knowingly, tread upon the meanest insect. But the Public Orator was a post of no mean calibre. His poem of *Lewesdon Hill* can never be read, but with admiration and delight.'

'Once in a large circle at New College, it was expected that he would show off before some strangers, who were tacitly invited to meet the author of *Lewesdon Hill*. Crowe sate silent a long time; it was in summer, and very hot. At last, unbuttoning nearly the whole of his waistcoat, and placing his arm within, and balancing himself in the see-saw action of his chair, the poet, looking out on the lawn, exclaimed, "Lud, lud! how green the grass looks!" These were the only words that escaped him during the symposium.' What his audience thought is not recorded.

On the many occasions as Public Orator when Crowe's talents were called upon, his orations were 'pregnant with classical spirit, gave the fullest evidence of his attainments as a scholar, nor did they degenerate into that tautology which the recurrence of similar topics is calculated to produce.' He was noted for his remarkable appearance on the rostrum, united to the powerful enunciation of his periods, and for his unfailing originality. He was also 'a good Latinist'. All his life he taught poetry, gave sermons and public lectures, and kept on walking the public highways. In addition to Alton Barnes he was rector of Llanymynech, between Oswestry and Welshpool, on the borders of Montgomeryshire and Shropshire and another parish in Yorkshire.

Samuel Rogers said: 'How little is Crowe known even to persons who are fond of poetry! Yet his *Lewesdon Hill* is full of noble passages.' Edmund Blunden simply noted that 'Crowe was of the William Barnes species', that is to say a clergyman-poet, both being much underrated. (Barnes, of course, wrote in Dorset dialect; Thomas Hardy owed much to his inspiration.) But Blunden also calls *Lewesdon Hill* 'masterly', and indeed both Wordsworth and Coleridge quickly recognised it as such, although it was never quite given its wider due.

Thus William Crowe was both a man of the cloth and a man of the world, one who was at home with timber, tobacco, brandy and corn, the ways of the land and of farming. It seems that in 1771 he discreetly married one Elizabeth Smith, a fruiterer's daughter; records show that a William Crowe married an Elizabeth Smith at Finmere, Oxford, on 11th November that year, and the coincidence seems too great to dismiss. In 1771, however, William was a young man of 26. Either he must have kept the marriage a secret, for as a Fellow he was not allowed by college statutes to be married, or else the authorities had learned to turn a blind eye.

William and his Elizabeth had seven children: three daughters, Louisa, Sophia and Matilda, and four sons, Frederick, William, George and Henry. William was an ensign in the 4th King's Own Regiment and was killed defending the colours at the disastrous battle of New Orleans on 8th January 1815. There is a memorial in the church at Alton Barnes, not only to Ensign William Crowe junior but also to his elder brother, Captain Frederick Crowe of the 1st Battalion of Pioneers, who died at Musulipatam in Andhra Pradesh, India, having fought in the Burma War, 1824–1826. The loss of both sons must have been a terrible blow.

'The Battle of New Orleans' has become a popular folk-song, and records the defeat of the British by an American force half its size. It was a rout. The British lost 385 killed, 1,186 wounded and 484 captured. The Americans only lost 13 killed, 58 wounded, 30 captured. It was the last battle of the 1812 war, but there is a double irony here: the Treaty of Ghent had actually been signed two weeks earlier, on 24th December 1814, both sides regarding the war as futile, but news of the peace would not reach New Orleans until February 1815. So the battle was pointless and unnecessary. And William Crowe senior was pro-republican and anti-militarist.

There are several contemporary accounts of Crowe, as well as one good sketch and a few paintings. He was not someone you forgot in a hurry. For a start he kept his broad Winchester accent and seemed to relish using it in his sermons and lectures, deploying the long 'a' to great effect from both pulpit and rostrum. But as the nineteenth century progressed he must have begun to seem an odd figure, a leftover of an earlier age, eclipsed by the likes of Byron, Coleridge, Wordsworth and Shelley. One wonders what Thomas de Quincey made of Crowe when he was up at Oxford in 1800's, for it was here that de Quincey started taking opium for his toothache.

Little is still known about Elizabeth Crowe, but in 1827 William's health deteriorated and he moved to Bath, where, by now nearly blind, he died two years later in February 1829, aged 84. He was buried at Alton Barnes. It is to be hoped that he was aware of his poetic influence, which came at a critical point for both Wordsworth and Coleridge. Now maybe it is time he was accorded the same degree of scholarship as those he inspired.

This is only a brief introduction but my hope is that many more people will come to appreciate William Crowe and the poem *Lewesdon Hill* for its simple beauty and keen observations. Hopefully they will use the poem not only to explore West Dorset and its fascinating history but to look at the poetic connections with the Romantic Movement, which blossomed after its timely publication. I expect Isaac Gulliver had a copy by his bedside, as well as a rummer filled with French brandy.

James Crowden – September 2007

LEWESDON HILL

A POEM.

Χαιρ' ω πεδον αγχιαλον,
Και μ' ευπλοια πεμψον αμεμπτως
Ενθ' η μεγαλη μοιρα κομιζει,
——————— χω πανδαματωρ
Δαιμων, ος ταυτ' επεκρανεν. SOPH.

Farewell thy printless sands and pebbly shore !
I hear the white surge beat thy coast no more,
Pure, gentle source of the high, rapturous mood !——
——— Wheree'er, like the great Flood, by thy dread force
Propell'd—shape Thou my calm, my blameless course,
Heaven, Earth and Ocean's Lord !—and Father of the Good !

* * *

BY WILLIAM CROWE, L.L.B. OF NEW COLLEGE
AND PUBLIC ORATOR OF THE UNIVERSITY.

THE SECOND EDITION.

OXFORD:
AT THE CLARENDON PRESS, MDCCLXXXVIII.
SOLD BY D. PRINCE AND J. COOKE, OXFORD:
J. F. AND C. RIVINGTON,
T. CADELL, AND R. FAULDER, LONDON.

TO THE

RIGHT REVEREND FATHER IN GOD

J O N A T H A N

LORD BISHOP OF ST. ASAPH

WHO IN A LEARNED FREE AND LIBERAL AGE

IS HIMSELF MOST HIGHLY DISTINGUISHED

BY EXTENSIVE USEFUL AND ELEGANT LEARNING

BY A DISINTERESTED SUPPORT OF FREEDOM

AND BY A TRULY CHRISTIAN LIBERALITY OF MIND

T H I S   P O E M

WITH ALL RESPECT IS DEDICATED

BY HIS LORDSHIP'S MOST OBLIGED

AND MOST OBEDIENT SERVANT

T H E   A U T H O R.

ADVERTISEMENT.

THE Hill which gives title to the following Poem is fituated in the weftern part of Dorfetfhire. This choice of a Subject, to which the Author was led by his refidence near the fpot, may feem perhaps to confine him to topics of mere rural and local defcription. But he begs leave here to inform the Reader that he has advanced beyond thofe narrow limits to fomething more general and important. On the other hand he trufts, that in his fartheft excurfions the connexion between him and his fubject will eafily be traced. The few notes which are fubjoined he thought neceffary to elucidate the paffages where they are inferted. He will only add in this place, from Hutchins's Hiftory of Dorfetfhire, (Vol. I. p. 366.) what is there faid of Lewefdon (or, as it is now corruptly called, Lewfon) ' This and Pillefdon Hill, ' furmount all the hills, though very high, between them ' and the fea. Mariners call them the *Cow and Calf*, in ' which forms they are fancied to appear, being eminent ' fea-marks to thofe who fail upon the coaft.'

To the top of this Hill the Author defcribes himfelf as walking on a May morning.

LEWESDON HILL.

UP to thy summit, LEWESDON, to the brow
Of yon proud rising, where the lonely thorn
Bends from the rude South-east, with top cut sheer
By his keen breath, along the narrow track
By which the scanty-pastured sheep ascend
Up to thy furze-clad summit, let me climb;
My morning exercise; and thence look round
Upon the variegated scene, of hills,
And woods, and fruitful vales, and villages
Half-hid in tufted orchards, and the sea
Boundless, and studded thick with many a sail.

Ye

Ye dew-fed vapours, nightly balm, exhaled
From earth, young herbs and flowers, that in the morn
Afcend as incenfe to the Lord of day,
I come to breathe your odours; while they float
Yet near this furface, let me walk embathed
In your invifible perfumes, to health
So friendly, nor lefs grateful to the mind,
Adminiftring fweet peace and cheerfulnefs.

How changed is thy appearance, beauteous hill!
Thou haft put off thy wintry garb, brown heath
And ruffet fern, thy feemly-colour'd cloak
To bide the hoary frofts and dripping rains
Of chill December, and art gaily robed
In livery of the fpring: upon thy brow
A cap of flowery hawthorn, and thy neck
Mantled with new-fprung furze and fpangles thick
Of golden bloom: nor lack thee tufted woods
Adown thy fides: Tall oaks of lufty green,
The darker fir, light afh, and the nefh tops
Of the young hazel join, to form thy fkirts

In

In many a wavy fold of verdant wreath.
So gorgeoufly hath Nature dreft thee up
Againft the birth of May ; and, vefted fo,
Thou doft appear more gracefully array'd
Than Fafhion's worfhippers ; whofe gaudy fhews,
Fantaftical as are a fick man's dreams,
From vanity to coftly vanity
Change ofter than the moon. Thy comely drefs,
From fad to gay returning with the year,
Shall grace thee ftill till Nature's felf fhall change.

Thefe are the beauties of thy woodland fcene
At each return of fpring : yet fome delight
Rather to view the change ; and fondly gaze
On fading colours, and the thoufand tints
Which Autumn lays upon the varying leaf.
I like them not ; for all their boafted hues
Are kin to Sicklinefs : mortal Decay
Is drinking up their vital juice ; that gone,
They turn to fear and yellow. Should I praife
Such falfe complexions, and for beauty take
A look confumption-bred ? As foon, if gray

Were

Were mixt in young Louifa's treffes brown,
I'd call it beautiful variety,
And therefore doat on her.   Yet I can fpy
A beauty in that fruitful change, when comes
The yellow Autumn and the hopes o'the year
Brings on to golden ripenefs; nor difpraife
The pure and fpotlefs form of that fharp time,
When January fpreads a pall of fnow
O'er the dead face of th'undiftinguifh'd earth.
Then ftand I in the hollow comb beneath
And blefs this friendly mount, that weather-fends
My reed-roof'd cottage, while the wintry blaft
From the thick north comes howling: till the Spring
Return, who leads my devious fteps abroad,
To climb, as now, to LEWESDON's airy top.

Above the noife and ftir of yonder fields
Uplifted, on this height I feel the mind
Expand itfelf in wider liberty.
The diftant founds break gently on my fenfe,
Soothing to meditation : fo methinks,
Even fo, fequefter'd from the noify world,

                                        Could

Could I wear out this tranfitory being
In peaceful contemplation and calm eafe.
But confcience, which ftill cenfures on our acts,
That awful voice within us, and the fenfe
Of an hereafter, wake and roufe us up
From fuch unfhaped retirement; which were elfe
A bleft condition on this earthy ftage.
For who would make his life a life of toil
For wealth, o'erbalanced with a thoufand cares;
Or power, which bafe compliance muft uphold;
Or honour, lavifh'd moft on courtly flaves;
Or fame, vain breath of a misjudging world;
Who for fuch perifhable gaudes would put
A yoke upon his free unbroken fpirit,
And gall himfelf with trammels and the rubs
Of this world's bufinefs; fo he might ftand clear
Of judgment and the tax of idlenefs
In that dread audit, when his mortal hours
(Which now with foft and filent ftealth pace by)
Muft all be counted for? But, for this fear,
And to remove, according to our power,
The wants and evils of our brother's ftate,

'Tis

'Tis meet we juftle with the world; content,
If by our fovereign Mafter we be found
At laft not profitlefs : for worldly meed,
Given or withheld, I deem of it alike.

From this proud eminence on all fides round
Th' unbroken profpect opens to my view ;
On all fides large ; fave only where the head
Of Pillefdon rifes, Pillefdon's lofty Pen :
So call (ftill rendering to his ancient name
Obfervance due) that rival Height fouth-weft,
Which like a rampire bounds the vale beneath.
There woods, there blooming orchards, there are feen
Herds, ranging, or at reft beneath the fhade
Of fome wide-branching oak; there goodly fields
Of corn, and verdant pafture, whence the kine
Returning with their milky treafure home
Store the rich dairy : fuch fair plenty fills
The pleafant vale of Marfhwood; pleafant now,
Since that the Spring has deck'd anew the meads
With flowery vefture, and the warmer fun
Their foggy moiftnefs drain'd; in wintry days

Cold,

Cold, vapourish, miry, wet, and to the flocks

Unfriendly, when autumnal rains begin

To drench the spungy turf: but ere that time

The careful shepherd moves to healthier soil,

Rechasing, lest his tender ewes should coath.*

In the dank pasturage.   Yet not the fields

Of *Evesham*, nor that ample valley named

Of the *White Horse*, its antique monument

Carved in the chalky bourne, for beauty' and wealth

Might equal, though surpassing in extent,

This fertile vale ; in length from LEWESDON's base

Extended to the sea, and water'd well

By many a rill ; but chief with thy clear stream,

Thou nameless Rivulet, who from the side

Of LEWESDON softly welling forth, dost trip

---

* To *coath*, Skinner says, is a word common in Lincolnshire ; and signifies, to *faint*. He derives it from the Anglo-Saxon, coðe, a *disease*. In Dorsetshire it is in common use, but is used of sheep only : a *coathed* sheep is a *rotten* sheep; to *coath* is to *take the rot*. *Rechasing* is also a term in that country appropriated to flocks : *to chase and rechase* is to drive sheep at certain times from one sort of ground to another, or from one parish to another.

The Author having ventured to introduce some provincial and other terms, takes this occasion to say, that it is a liberty in which he has not indulged himself, but when he conceived them to be allowable for the sake of ornament or expression.

Adown

Adown the valley, wandering fportively.
Alas, how foon thy little courfe will end!
How foon thy infant ftream fhall lofe itfelf
In the falt mafs of waters, ere it grow
To name or greatnefs! Yet it flows along
Untainted with the commerce of the world,
Nor paffing by the noify haunts of men;
But through fequefter'd meads, a little fpace,
Winds fecretly, and in its wanton path
May cheer fome drooping flower, or minifter
Of its cool water to the thirfty lamb:
Then falls into the ravenous fea, as pure
As when it iffued from its native hill.

So to thine early grave didft thou run on,
Spotlefs Francefca, fo, after fhort courfe,
Thine innocent and playful infancy
Was fwallowed up in death, and thy pure fpirit
In that illimitable gulph which bounds
Our mortal continent. But not there loft,
Not there extinguifh'd, as fome falfely teach,
Who can talk much and learnedly of life,

Who

Who know our frame and fashion, who can tell
The substance and the properties of man,
As they had seen him made; aye and stood by
Spies on Heaven's work. They also can discourse
Wisely, to prove that what must be must be,
And shew how thoughts are jogg'd out of the brain
By a mechanical impulse; pushing on
The minds of us, poor unaccountables,
To fatal resolution. Know they not,
That in this mortal life, whate'er it be,
We take the path that leads to good or evil,
And therein find our bliss or misery?
And this includes all reasonable ends
Of knowledge or of being; farther to go
Is toil unprofitable, and th' effect
Most perilous wandering. Yet of this be sure;
Where Freedom is not, there no Virtue is:
If there be none, this world is all a cheat,
And the divine stability of Heaven
(That assured seat for good men after death)
Is but a transient cloud; display'd so fair
To cherish virtuous hope, but at our need

C

Eludes

Eludes the fenfe, and fools our honeft faith,
Vanifhing in a lie. If this be fo,
Were it not better to be born a beaft,
Only to feel what is, and thus to fcape
The aguifh fear that fhakes the afflicted breaft
With fore anxiety of what fhall be ;
And all for nought ? Since our moft wicked act
Is not our fin, and our religious awe
Delufion ; if that ftrong Neceffity
Chains up our will. But that the mind is free,
The Mind herfelf, beft judge of her own ftate,
Is feelingly convinced ; nor to be moved
By fubtle words, that may perplex the head,
But ne'er perfuade the heart. Vain Argument,
That with falfe weapons of Philofophy
Fights againft Hope, and Senfe, and Nature's ftrength !

See how the Sun, here clouded, afar off
Pours down the golden radiance of his light
Upon the enridged fea ; where the black fhip
Sails on the phofphor-feeming waves. So fair,
But falfely-flattering, was yon furface calm,

When

When forth for India fail'd in evil time
That Veffel whofe difaftrous fate, when told,
Fill'd every breaft with horror, and each eye
With piteous tears; fo cruel was the lofs.†
Methinks I fee her, as, by the wintry ftorm
Shatter'd and driven along paft yonder Ifle,
She ftrove, her lateft hope, by ftrength or art
To gain the Port within it, or at worft
To fhun that harbourlefs and hollow coaft

† The diftrefsful condition of the Halfwell here alluded to is
thus circumftantially defcribed in the Narrative of her lofs, p. 13.
"Thurfday the 5th, at two in the morning the wind came to
the fouthward, blew frefh, and the weather was very thick: at
noon Portland was feen, bearing N. by E. diftance two or three
leagues; at eight at night it blew a ftrong gale at S. and at this
time the Portland lights were feen, bearing N.W. diftance four
or five leagues, when they wore fhip, and got her head to the
weftward; but finding they loft ground upon that tack, they
wore again, and kept ftretching on eaftward, in hopes to have
weathered Peverel-point, in which cafe they intended to have an-
chored in Studland Bay: at 11 at night it cleared, and they faw
St. Alban's-head a mile and a half to the leeward of them; upon
which they took in fail immediately, and let go the fmall bower
anchor, which brought up the fhip at a whole cable, and fhe rode
for about an hour, but then drove; they now let go the fheet an-
chor and wore away a whole cable, and the fhip rode for about
two hours longer, when fhe drove again.—They were then driving
very faft on fhore, and might expect every moment to ftrike."

From

From Portland eaftward to the * Promontory,
Where ftill St. Alban's high-built chapel ftands.
But art nor ftrength avail her : on fhe drives,
In ftorm and darknefs to the fatal coaft;
And there 'mong rocks and high-o'erhanging cliffs
Dafh'd piteoufly, with all her precious freight
Was loft ; by Neptune's wild and foamy jaws
Swallow'd up quick ! The richlieft-laden fhip
Of fpicy Ternate, or that annual, fent
To the Philippines o'er the Southern main
From Acapulco, carrying maffy gold,
Were poor to this ;—freighted with hopeful Youth,
And Beauty, and high Courage undifmay'd
By mortal terrors, and paternal Love,

* ' Not far from this (Encombe) ftands St. *Aldene's* Chapel :
which took name from the dedication to St. Adeline, the firft Bi-
fhop of Sherbourne in this fhire : but now it ferves for a fea-
mark.' Coker's Survey of Dorfetfh. p. 47.
    Near the fea is the high land of *St. Aldhelm's*, commonly called
St. Alban's, a noted fea-mark. The cliff here is 147 yards per-
pendicular. On this promontory, about a mile S. of *Worth*,
ftands a chapel of the fame name.' Hutchins's Dorfetfh. Vol. I.
p. 228. But this head-land is not marked by name in Hutchins's
map. ' The very utter part of *St. Aldhelm's* point is five miles
from *Sandwich (Swandich.)* Lel. Itin. Vol. III. p. 53.

Strong

Strong, and unconquerable even in death—
Alas, they perish'd all, all in one hour!

Now yonder high way view, wide-beaten, bare
With ceaseless tread of men and beasts, and track
Of many' indenting wheels, heavy and light,
That violently rush with unsafe speed,
Or slowly turn, oft-resting, up the steep.
Mark how that road, with mazes serpentine,
From * Shipton's bottom to the lofty down
Winds like a path of pleasure, drawn by art
Through park or flowery garden for delight.
Nor less delightful this; if, while he mounts
Not wearied, the free Journeyer will pause
To view the prospect oft, as oft to see
Beauty still changing: yet not so contrived.
By fancy' or choice, but of necessity,
By soft gradations of ascent to lead

* Shipton is a hill, which, according to common report, is so
called from it's shape : the top of it being formed like a ship with
the keel upwards. It stands three miles from Bridport on the road
towards London; which road passes by the foot of it to the
North.

The

The labouring and way-worn feet along,
And make their toil lefs toilfome.   Half way up
Or nearer to the top, behold a cot,
O'er which the branchy trees, thofe fycamores,
Wave gently: at their roots a ruftic bench
Invites to fhort refrefhment, and to tafte
What grateful beverage the houfe may yield
After fatigue, or dufty heat; thence call'd
The *Traveller's Reft*. Welcome, embower'd feat,
Friendly repofe to the flow paffenger
Afcending, ere he takes his fultry way
Along th' interminable road, ftretch'd out
Over th' unfhelter'd down; or when at laft
He has that hard and folitary path
Meafured by painful fteps. And bleft are they,
Who in life's toilfome journey may make paufe
After a march of glory : yet not fuch
As rife in caufelefs war, troubling the world
By their mad quarrel, and in fields of blood
Hail'd victors, thence renown'd, and call'd on earth
Kings, heroes, demi-gods, but in high Heaven
Theives, ruffians, murderers; thefe find no repofe :

                                        Thee

Thee rather, patriot Conqueror, to thee
Belongs fuch reft; who in the weftern world,
Thine own deliver'd country, for thyfelf
Haft planted an immortal grove, and there
Upon the glorious mount of Liberty
Repofing, fit'ft beneath the palmy fhade.

And Thou, not lefs renown'd in like attempt
Of high atchievement, though thy virtue fail'd
To fave thy little country, Patriot Prince,
Hero, Philofopher (what more could they
Who wifely chofe Thee, PAOLI, to blefs
Thy native Ifle, long ftrugling to be free?
But Heaven allow'd not) yet may'ft thou repofe
After thy glorious toil, fecure of fame
Well-earn'd by virtue: while ambitious France,
Who ftretch'd her lawlefs hand to feize thine ifle,
Enjoys not reft or glory; with her prey
Gorged but not fatisfied, and craving ftill
Againft th' intent of Nature. See Her now
Upon the adverfe fhore, her Norman coaft,

Plying

* Plying her monftrous labour unreftrain'd;
A rank of caftles in the rough fea funk,
With towery fhape and height, and armed heads
Uprifing o'er the furge; and thefe between,
Unmeafurable mafs of ponderous rock
Projected many a mile to rear her wall
Midft the deep waters. She, the mighty work
Still urging, in her arrogant attempt,
As with a lordly voice to the Ocean cries,
' Hitherto come, no farther; here be ftaid
' The raging of thy waves; within this bound
' Be all my haven:' and therewith takes in
A fpace of ampleft circuit, wide and deep,
Won from the ftraiten'd main: nor lefs in ftrength
Than in dimenfions; giant-like in both:
On each fide flank'd with citadels and towers
And rocky walls, and arches maffy proof
Againft the ftorm of war. Compared with this,
† Lefs, and lefs hazardous emprize atcheived

---

* A detail of this vaft project is given at the conclufion of this Poem.

† Quin. Curt. lib. 4. cap. 2, 3.

Refiftlefs

Refiftlefs Alexander, when he caft
The ftrong foundations of that high-raifed mound
Deep in the hoftile waves, his martial way,
Built on before him up to fea-girt Tyre.
* Nor aught fo bold, fo vaft, fo wonderful,
At Athos or the fetter'd Hellefpont,
Imagined in his pride that Afian vain,
Xerxes,—but ere he turn'd from Salamis
Fly'ing through the blood-red waves in one poor bark,
Retarded by thick-weltering carcaffes.
† Nor yet that elder work (if work it were,
Not fable) raifed upon the Phrygian fhore,
(Where lay the fleet confederate againft Troy,
A thoufand fhips behind the vafty mole
All fhelter'd) could with this compare, though built
It feem'd, of greatnefs worthy to create
Envy in the immortals ; and at laft
Not overthrown without th' embattled aid
Of angry Neptune. So may He once more
Rife from his troubled bed, and fend his waves,

* Juv. Sat. X. v. 173, 186.
† Hom. Il. VII. v. 433, 463. et Il. XII. v. 1, 33.

Urged

Urged on to fury by contending winds,
With horned violence to push and whelm
This pile, usurping on his watry reign!

From hostile shores returning, glad I look
On native scenes again; and first salute
Thee, * Burton, and thy lofty cliff, where oft
The nightly blaze is kindled; further seen
Than erst was that love-tended cresset, hung
Beside the Hellespont: yet not like that
Inviting to the hospitable arms
Of Beauty' and Youth, but lighted up, the sign
Of danger, and of ambush'd foes to warn
The stealth-approaching Vessel, homeward bound
From Havre or the Norman isles, with freight
Of wines and hotter drinks, the trash of France,
Forbidden merchandize. Such fraud to quell
Many a light skiff and well-appointed sloop

---

* Burton is a village near the Sea, lying S. E. from Lewes-
don, and about two miles S. of Shipton-hill beforementioned.
The Cliff is among the loftiest of all upon that coast; and
Smugglers often take advantage of its height for the purpose re-
lated in the poem.

Lies

Lies hovering near the coaſt, or hid behind
Some curved promontory, in hope to ſeize
Theſe contraband : vain hope ! on that high ſhore,
Station'd, th' aſſociates of their lawleſs trade
Keep watch, and to their fellows off at ſea
Give the known ſignal ; they with fearful haſte
Obſervant, put about the ſhip, and plunge
Into concealing darkneſs. As a fox,
That from the cry of hounds and hunters' din
Runs crafty down the wind, and ſteals away
Forth from his cover, hopeful ſo t' elude
The not yet following pack,—if chance the ſhout
Of eager or unpractiſed boy betray
His meditated flight, back he retires
To ſhelter him in the thick wood : ſo theſe
Retiring, ply to ſouth, and ſhun the land
Too perilous to approach : and oft at ſea
Secure (or ever nigh the guarded coaſt
They venture) to the trackleſs deep they truſt
Their forfeitable cargo, rundlets ſmall,
Together link'd upon their cable's length,
And to the ſhelving bottom ſunk and fixt

By

By ftony weights; till happier hour arrive
To land it on the vacant beach unrifk'd.

But what is yonder † Hill, whofe dufky brow
Wears, like a regal diadem, the round
Of antient battlements and ramparts high ;
And frowns upon the vales ? I know thee not.
Thou haft no name, no honourable note,
No chronicle of all thy warlike pride,
To teftify what once thou wert, how great,
How glorious, and how fear'd. So perifh all,

---

† ' Eggardon Hill is a very high hill, and gives name to the
Hundred. Mr. Coker fays it is uncertain whether it takes its
name from Edgar, King of the Weft Saxons, or from Orgarus,
Earl of Cornwall : and indeed this laft derivation is the trueft ;
there being little reafon to doubt that it is the old *Orgareftone*.
The camp on the brow of this hill is a large and ftrong fortifi-
cation, and feems to be Roman.' Hutchins's Dorfet. Vol. I. p.
289 ; where there is an engraving of this camp. But Hutchins has
mifreprefented Mr. Coker, who indeed prefers the derivation from
Orgar. His words are thefe : ' That it takes name from Edgar,
the Weft Saxon King, I dare not affirm, having nothing to prove
it but the nearneffe of the name. It better likes me to think this
the place, which in Doomfday-book is called Orgarefton, but
whether it take name from Orgareus, Earl of Cornwall, I know
not ; though I think I fhould run into no great error to believe it.'
Coker's Survey of Dorfetfhire, p. 26.

Who.

Who feek their greatnefs in dominion held
Over their fellows, or the pomp of war;
And be as thou forgotten, and their fame
Cancell'd like thine! But thee in after times
Reclaim'd to culture, Shepherds vifited,
And call'd thee Orgarfton; fo thee they call'd
Of Orgar, Saxon earl, the wealthy fire
Of fair Elfrida; She, whofe happy Bard
Has with his gentle witchery fo wrought
Upon our fenfe, that we can fee no more
Her mad ambition, treacherous cruelty,
And purple robes of ftate with royal blood
Inhofpitably ftain'd; but in their place
Pure faith, foft manners, filial duty meek,
Connubial love, and ftoles of faintly white.

Fain would I view thee, Corfcombe, fain would hail
The ground where * Hollis lies; his choice retreat,

* 'Mr. Hollis, in order to preferve the memory of thofe he-
roes and patriots for whom he had a veneration, as the affertors
and defenders of his country, called many of the farms and fields
in his eftate at Corfcombe by their names; and by thefe names
they are ftill diftinguifhed. In the middle of one of thofe fields,
not far from his houfe, he ordered his corps to be depofited in a
grave

Where, from the bufy world withdrawn, he lived

To generous Virtue and the holy love

Of Liberty, a dedicated fpirit:

And left his afhes there; ftill honouring

Thy fields, with title given of patriot names,

But more with his untitled fepulchre.

That envious ridge conceals thee from my fight;

Which, paffing o'er thy place north-eaft, looks on

To Sherburne's ancient towers and rich domains,

The noble Digby's manfion; where he dwells

Inviolate, and fearlefs of thy curfe,

War-glutted * Ofmund, fuperftitious Lord!

grave ten feet deep; and that the field fhould be immediately plowed over, that no trace of his burial place might remain.' Memoirs of Thomas Hollis, Efq. Vol. I. p. 481.

* Of the ftrange Curfe belonging to Shireburne-Caftle. From a MS. of the late Bifhop of Ely (Bp John More) now in the Royal Library at Cambridge.

'Ofmund a Norman Knight (who had ferved *William* Duke of *Normandy* from his youth, in all his wars againft the French King, and the Duke's (*William*'s) fubjects, with much valour and difcretion) for all his faithful fervice (when his Mafter had by conqueft obteyned the crown of England) was rewarded with many great gifts; among the which was the Earldome of *Dorfett*, and the gift of many other Poffeffions, whereof the Caftle and Baronie of *Sherburne* were parcell. But Ofmund, in the declyninge of his age, calling to mynde the great effufion of blood, which, from

his

Who with Heaven's juſtice for a bloody life

Madeſt thy preſumptuous bargain ; giving more

his infancie, he had ſhedd; he reſolved to leave all worldly
delights, and betake himſelf to a religious life, the better to
contemplate on his former ſinnes and to obteyn Pardon for them.
And with much importunitie, having got leave of the Kinge
(who was unwilling to want the aſſiſtance of ſo grave and worthy
a Counſeller) to reſign his temporall honors ; and having obteyned
the Biſhoprick of *Sarum*, he gave *Sherburne* with other lands to
the Biſhoprick. To which gift he annexed this Curſe,

That whoſoever ſhould take thoſe Lands from the Biſhoprick,
or diminiſh them in great or in ſmall, ſhould be accurſed,
not only in this world, but alſo in the world to come; un-
leſs in his life-time he made reſtitution thereof. And ſo
he died Biſhop of Sarum.

Thoſe lands continued in the poſſeſſion of his ſucceſſors till the
reign of King Stephen, who took them away ; ' whereupon (ſays
this Account) his proſperity forſook him.' King Stephen being
dead, ' theſe lands came into the hands of ſome of the *Moun-
tagues* (after Erles of *Sarum*) who whileſt they held the ſame, un-
derwent many diſaſters. For one or other of them fell by misfor-
tune. And finally, all the males of them became extinct, and the
Earldome received an end in their name. So ill was their ſucceſs.'

After this the lands were reſtored to the Biſhoprick; but were
taken away a ſecond time by the Duke of Somerſet, in the reign
of Edward VI; ' when the Duke, being hunting in the Parke
of *Sherburne*, he was ſent for preſently unto the Kinge (to whome
he was Protector) and at his coming up to *Landon*, was forth-
with committed unto the *Tower*, and, ſhortly after, loſt his head.'
The lands then, in a ſuit at law, were adjudged to the Biſhop of
Sarum ; and ſo remained, ' till Sir Walter Raleigh procured a grant
of them ; he afterwards unfortunately loſt them, and at laſt his head
alſo. Upon his attainder they came, by the King's gift, to Prince

Henry ;

Than thy juft having to redeem thy guilt,

And daredft bid th' Almighty to become

The minifter of thy curfe. But fure it fell,

So bigots fondly judged, full fure it fell

With facred vengeance pointed on the head

Of many a bold ufurper: chief on thine

(Favourite of Fortune once but laft her thrall)

Accomplifh'd * Raleigh! in that lawlefs day

Henry; who died not long after the poffeffion thereof. After Prince *Henry's* death, the Erle of *Somerfett (Carr)* did poffeffe them. Finally, he loft them, and many other greater fortunes.' Peck's Defid. Cur. Lib. 14. No. 6.

    * ' How Dr. *John Coldwell,* of a Phyfitian became a Bifhop I have heard by more than a good many; and I will briefly handle it, and as tenderly as I can; bearing myfelf equal between the living (Sir *Walter Raleigh)* and the dead (Bifhop *Coldwell*). Yet the manifeft judgments of God on both of them I may not pafs over with filence. And to fpeak firft of the Knight, who carried off the *Spolia Opima* of the Bifhoprick. He having gotten *Sherborne* Caftle, Park, and Parfonage, was in thofe days in fo great favour with the Queen, as I may boldly fay, that with lefs fuit than he was fain to make to her e'er he could perfect this his purchafe, and with lefs money than he beftowed fince in *Sherborne* (in building and buying out leafes, and in drawing the river through rocks into his garden) he might, very juftly, and without offence of either Church or State, have compaffed a much better purchafe. Alfo, as I have been truly informed, he had a prefage before he firft attempted it, which did forfhew it would turn to his ruin, and might have kept him from meddling with it,—*Si mens non læva fuiffet*: For as he was riding poft between

Plymouth

When, like a goodly hart, thou wert befet
With crafty blood-hounds lurching for thy life
Whileas they feign'd to chace thee fairly down:
And that foul Scot, the minion-kiffing king,
Purfued with havoc in the tyrannous hunt.

How is it vanifh'd in a hafty fpleen,
The Tor of Glaftonbury! Even but now

Plymouth and the Court [as many times he did upon no fmall em-
ployments) this Caftle being right in the way, he caft fuch an eye
upon it as *Ahab* did upon *Naboth*'s Vineyard. And, once above
the reft, being talking of it (of the commodioufnefs of the place,
of the ftrength of the feat, and how eafily it might be got from
the Bifhopric) fuddenly over and over came his horfe, that his very
face (which was then thought a very good face) plowed up the
earth where he fell. This fall was ominous I make no queftion;
and himfelf was apt to conftrue it fo. But his brother *Adrian*
would needs have him interpret it as a conqueror, that his fall
prefaged the quiet poffeffion of it. And accordingly for the prefent
it fo fell out. So that with much labor, travel, coft, envy, and
obloquy he got it *habendum et tenendum* to him and his heirs. But
fee what became of him. In the public joy and jubile of the
whole realm (when favor, peace, and pardon, were offered
even to offenders) he who in wit, in wealth, in courage was infe-
rior to few, fell fuddenly (I cannot tell how) into fuch a down-
fall of defpair, as his greateft enemy would not have wifhed him
fo much harm, as he would have done himfelf. Can any man
be fo wilfully blind, as not to fee and fay, *Digitus Dei hic eft!*"
Harrington's Breif View, p. 88.

E   I

I faw the hoary pile crefting the top
Of that north-weftern hill; and in this Now
A cloud hath paft on it, and its dim bulk
Becomes annihilate, or if not, a fpot
Which the ftrain'd vifion tires itfelf to find.

And even fo fares it with the things of earth
Which feem moft conftant: there will come the cloud
That fhall infold them up, and leave their place
A feat for Emptinefs. Our narrow ken
Reaches too far, when all that we behold
Is but the havoc of wide-wafting Time,
Or what he foon fhall fpoil. His out-fpread wings
(Which bear him like an eagle o'er the earth)
Are plumed in front fo downy foft they feem
To fofter what they touch, and mortal fools
Rejoice beneath their hovering: woe the while!
For in that indefatigable flight
The multitudinous ftrokes inceffantly
Bruife all beneath their cope, and mark on all
His fecret injury; on the front of man
Gray hairs and wrinkles; ftill as Time fpeeds on
Hard and more hard his iron pennons beat

                                                With

With ceafelefs violence; nor overpafs,
Till all the creatures of this nether world
Are one wide quarry : following dark behind,
The cormorant Oblivion fwallows up
The carcaffes that Time has made his prey.

But hark ! the village clock ftrikes nine; the chimes
Merrily follow, tuneful to the fenfe
Of the pleafed clown attentive, while they make
Falfe-meafured melody on crazy bells.
O wondrous Power of modulated found !
Which like the air (whofe all-obedient fhape
Thou makeft thy flave) canft fubtilly pervade
The yielded avenues of fenfe, unlock
The clofe affections, by fome fairy path
Winning an eafy way through every ear,
And with thine unfubftantial quality
Holding in mighty chains the hearts of all ;
All, but fome cold and fullen-temper'd fpirits,
Who feel no touch of fympathy or love.

Yet what is mufic, and the blended power
Of voice with inftruments of wind and ftring ?

What

What but an empty pageant of sweet noise?
Tis past: and all that it has left behind
Is but an echo dwelling in the ear
Of the toy-taken fancy, and beside
A void and countless hour in life's brief day.

But ill accords my verse with the delights
Of this gay month: and see the Villagers
Assembling jocund in their best attire
To grace this genial morn. Now I descend
To join the worldly croud; perchance to talk,
To think, to act as they: then all these thoughts,
That lift th' expanded heart above this spot
To heavenly musing, these shall pass away
(Even as this goodly prospect from my view)
Hidden by near and earthy-rooted cares.
So passeth human life; our better mind
Is as a sunday's garment, then put on
When we have nought to do; but at our work
We wear a worse for thrift. Of this enough:
To-morrow for severer thought; but now
To breakfast, and keep festival to-day.

T H E   E N D.

[See page 16.—THE works now carrying on at Cherburgh to make a haven for ſhips of war, are principally the following. Of theſe however it is not intended to give a full deſcription; but only to mention ſome particulars, from which an idea may be formed of the greatneſs of the ſcheme.

In the open ſea, above a league from the town and within half a mile weſt of a rock called *L'iſle Pelée*, a pier is begun, with deſign of conducting it on to the ſhore ſomewhat beyond *Point Hommet*, about two miles weſtward of Cherburgh. In order to this, a ſtrong frame of timber-work, of the ſhape of a truncated cone, having been conſtructed on the beach, was buoyed out, and ſunk in a depth of water; which at loweſt ebb is 35 feet, and where the tide riſes near 20 feet. The diameter of this cone at bottom is about 60 yards, its height 70 feet; and the area on its top large enough to receive a battery of cannon, with which it is hereafter to be fortified. Its ſolid contents are 2500 French toiſes; which in our meaſure (allowiug the French foot to be to the Engliſh as 144 to 135) will amount to 24,250 cubic yards nearly. Several other cones, of equal dimenſions, are ſunk at convenient diſtances from each other; forming the line of the pier: their number, when complete, it is ſaid, will be forty. As ſoon as any one of theſe is carried to its place, it is filled with ſtones, which are dug from mount *Rouille* and other rocks near the coaſt, and brought on horſes to the ſhore; whence they are conveyed to the cones in veſſels of forty, ſixty, or eighty tons burden. In like manner, but with much greater labour and expence, the ſpaces between the cones are filled up with ſtones thrown looſely into the ſea, till the heap is raiſed above the water. On this maſs, as on a foundation, a wall of maſonry-work is to be erected. The length of the whole is near five miles. On *L'iſle Pelée* and *Point Hommet*, before-mentioned, large fortifications are conſtructed bomb-proof to defend the Haven and Pier. It is the opinion of ſome perſons that this ſtupendous mole may be injured or deſtroyed by what is called a ground-ſea: *i. e.* a ſea when the waters are agitated to the bottom: and this happens, when a ſtrong wind, after having put the waves in motion, ſuddenly ſhifts to the oppoſite quarter. The deſcription given in the Poem of this vaſt undertaking cloſes with an alluſion to this opinion.]

Acknowledgements

My thanks to Richard Watkins of Barrington for finding an original copy of the 1788 edition of *Lewesdon Hill*, to John Roberts of Stoke Abbot and Roger Peers of Beaminster for sharing their research on William Crowe. The wonderful names of Thomas Hollis's farms and fields came from *A History of Halstock* by Pam Lemmey. The smuggling information comes from *Dorset Smugglers* by Roger Guttridge. *The Halsewell* and *Earl of Abergavenny* information comes from *Dorset Shipwrecks* by Maureen Attwooll published by The Dovecote Press.

Also of interest is *Dorset Worthies No5* William Crowe, by Edmund Blunden, published by the Dorset Natural History and Archaeological Society. One very useful essay on Coleridge and Crowe appeared in *The Modern Language Review*, Vol. 62, No. 3 (Jul., 1967), by C. G. Martin.

The Introduction to the Woodstock Press 1989 reprint of *Lewesdon Hill* written by Professor Jonathan Wordsworth is also well worth a squint as it focuses on William Wordsworth and Crowe.

William Crowe's obituary appeared in the *Gentleman's Magazine* 1829 and Thomas Frognal Dibdin's recollections of the man himself appeared in the 1836 volume. Also of use: biographical details in the Oxford DNB.

My thanks also go to the National Portrait Gallery for allowing the use of their 1808 hand-coloured etching of William Crowe by Robert Dighton.

My thanks to John Roberts, Caroline Carless and Carol Trewin for sterling work proof reading and editing. Thanks to Andrew Crane for designing the re-print and to Remous Ltd of Milborne Port for printing.